C2108(

CW00763497

0 6 MAR 2019

WHAT THEY LEFT BEHIND

SUE DYMOKE

Shoestring Press

Printed by imprintdigital
Upton Pyne, Exeter
www.digital.imprint.co.uk

Typesetting and cover design by narrator
www.narrator.me.uk
info@narrator.me.uk
033 022 300 39

Published by Shoestring Press
19 Devonshire Avenue, Beeston, Nottingham, NG9 1BS
(0115) 925 1827
www.shoestringpress.co.uk

First published 2018
© Copyright: Sue Dymoke
© Cover photo by Sue Dymoke

The moral right of the author has been asserted.

ISBN 978-1-912524-08-2

ACKNOWLEDGEMENTS

Thanks are due to the editors of the following books, journals and newspapers in which a number of these poems, or versions of these poems, first appeared: *Brittle Star*, *English in Education*, *Ekphrastic Review*, *LeftLion*, *Litter*, *Welcome to Leicester: poems about the city* (Dahlia Books); *New Walk*; *Raceme*; *Stride*, *Strike up the Band: poems for John Lucas at 80* (Plas Gwyn Books); *The Golden Shovel Anthology* (The University of Arkansas Press); *The Interpreter's House*, *The North*; *Under the Radar*.

A version of the poem 'Arboretum Shapes' won the *Nottingham Green Spaces Poetry Competition* in 2016.

The poems 'Oranges', 'At Ryoanji Temple' and 'What they left behind' were begun in Japan in December 2017. I would like to thank Yuka Nakai, The University of Hiroshima and the Japanese Society for the Promotion of Science for making our visit possible.

for Dave, always

CONTENTS

SMALL REBUS

Things we saved
things we lost
things we never had
collage past and imagined life
congruence and separation.

Candy-striped sheets
cotton for summer
bobbled winceyette for winter
comforting lines
thin and thick
purple, pink
orange, green,
red and blue
rainbows made
by undercover torchlight
in silent reading dark.

Photographs of days
we half remembered
or memories made only
by photographs stuffed
into faded Kodachrome envelopes.
Blue-silk bridesmaids in a muddy churchyard
black and white sea-front walks
with a long-gone grandad
half cousins in dark houses
with mantelpieces we don't recognise.

Tarnished cups, navy patent-leather shoes
that can never be buffed
to their former shine.
Teddy bears with chipped eyes and
a final moulting of fur.
Bedtime stories we listened to

over and over and
their vanished covers.

Small things still puzzle away.
Their colours never
quite match up.

GIRLS ON SWINGS

(After *Girls on Swings, Leeds 1953* by Roger Mayne)

Stretch out your feet

Kick your heels

Surge through sky

Push yourself higher

Be alive in that space

its rush of free air

all of your own making

MONARCH OF THE BEST ROOM

Even if you only open the door a fraction,
send a slither of light and backroom fug
across wrapped glass and best china
you will catch his stern eye.
The Monarch of the Glen stares out
across Little Gran's best room
from his prime position over a sideboard
beside chimney breast and unlit hearth.

The stag holds you in his gaze
while you try to remember
what must be fetched from
her shrouded place, rarely used
except when great aunts from Staines
call for special Sunday teas or
a sudden sadness shudders open
the front door, draws back heavy curtains
to let the mourners in.

Landseer's Monarch seems at home
in his enforced double gloaming.
Not that there's any glen grandeur here.
No antlered majesty roams through
these heather-free allotments, bracken-less ginnels
with their outside lavs, leftover Anderson shelters,
borders of frothy London Pride.
The only local fauna a squabble of geese
scolding dogs and blue budgies who flit
across backyard cages,
scrape on cuttlefish bone
chirruping in spite of it all.

THEIR PINNIES

They were always in their household armour
Mum, both grans.

Little Gran's was sprigged
with red and blue forget me-nots
bordered by navy ticking.
Soft white cotton
matched her soft white hair,
wrapped fully around her thin frame
tied at the back.

Big Gran's was more of an overall
ochre or maybe brown
stretching over her wide bosom
broad shoulders, mottled arms
stirring Boxing Day turkey broth
wide pans of chutneys, plum jams.

Mum's pinnies changed over the decades,
and from weekdays to Sunday best.
A sixties' yellow red abstract pattern
for dinners, teas and those endless sandwiches,
a decorative, dark green half-pinny with triangular pockets
for Sunday servings: egg salad,
Dundee cake, tinned cling peaches (with cream).
Her late seventies' look was navy butcher's stripe
tied at the front, its serious cream tapes
suiting her only foray into
continental cheffery: beef and red wine casserole
made with cooking wine bought
specially in tiny bottles from Boots the Chemists.

Never ever worn by men,
their pinnies saw hard labour
soaked up stains and tears, smudges and smells
beetroot blood and blackberries,
hairdresser's purple *Vitapoint* and piccalilli,
cradled colanders of sliced runner beans,
conjured up Saturday stew, bread pudding
sweet apple tart, liver and onions.

In the end, all her other clothes went
after a week of charity shop trips—
even the "beaver" coat
she'd saved for rare posh dos—
but her pinny, the yellow red abstract
of sausages on sticks and mandarin jellies
roast potatoes and comforting rhubarb crumble
folded itself away
in their dressing table drawer.

I put it back quick.

THE *PRIMROSA* PLATE

With its uneven fluted edges
her small *Primrosa*
formed part of an irregular set
of yellow plates, cups and saucers
at Big Gran's each Sunday teatime.

Less creamy, yellower than ridged china
from a newer *Woods* service
the plate held a slice of dark fruit cake
its cherries deeply submerged
or a very crumbly scone, thick with butter,
homemade blackcurrant.

Sunday's plate always doubled as Monday's.
Leftover Yorkshire pudding eaten
cold with a splodge of jam after
her kitchen floor was swept
horse brasses polished,
first wash through the wringer.

The plate cracked in three large pieces
many unsalvageable others,
last brightness from a long-gone room
where she sits at her half-moon table
when I come around the corner
rest my bike handles on the window ledge
peer in.

TIME AND MOTION

Time is money, in the hands of the managers: Jeremy Deller, 2014

At its beck and call
all his working life
he is never lost to time.
The twelve noon chase home
up across the railway bridge
his but one of a grimacing swarm of black
bicycles scenting dinner at half a mile:
table set, tea brewing
boiled potatoes on their last revolve.

Now the TV schedule shapes his days.
He knows the programme codes,
is irritated by their unannounced changes.
He eats between halves, or matches or innings,
never answers the phone after six
when only strangers would call.
His forty years' long service gift
ticks over the gas fire,
thirty years on.

ROAMING RANGE

You roamed wherever your bikes took you
where blackberries grew big and juicy
on railway cuttings, river banks, sunny field edges
where ploughs skirted hedgerows
where bedraggled ribbons mixed
with a must of grass clippings and wreath remnants
heaped near the graveyard tap
where rabbits scuttled into siding burrows
and conkers, released from spiked flails,
gleamed on rutted pathways
where out-of-sight cross-country runners
slowed to a smoking stroll
where a nettle's sting was only
partly eased by spit-rub of dock leaf
where tadpoles jellied in deep ponds
and bluebells chimed silent songs
under greening beeches
where hair snared in thickets
goose grass stuck to jumpers
brambles snagged anoraks
in dank misting twilight
where nobody knew where you were
but home was a quick ride away
when the lure of bangers and mash
became too strong to resist.

I KNOW THIS CITY

Nottingham, Saturday November 21st, 2015

I know this city.

I know that Yates's Wine Lodge
(where the Australian wine liquor is like no other)
is still Yates's
even though the Friends' Trio no longer plays here.

I know that the left lion is
the best place to meet
while the right lion stares enviously,
forever the loner.

I know that strictly no confetti can be thrown
on the Council House steps,
the Christmas market arrives too early each Autumn
and will, once more, outstay its welcome.

I now know that ostrich burgers, reindeer steaks
and Lincolnshire Poacher are traditional Xmas flavours
and you can buy reusable snow
or a 99 cornet in late November.

I know that Nottingham people
can seem reserved
or suspicious even
before they welcome you.

I know they like to drink and plan
their stages of inebriation over a lunchtime natter
a first pint, a cheeky glass of fizz to pep up
their afternoon endeavour.

I know this city is in early winter:
plane trees have lost their leaf loads
and first frosts crust windscreen and pavement.

I know that the laughter in here is getting louder
and glitter-topped twenty-somethings cluster
round their Primark bags, draining glasses,
urging their barman to *get a shift on.*

I know that some of their future other halves
have headed sofa-wards to big screen
BTSKY pre-match reports, league tables, speculation
and plenty of banter.

I know that the warming fug of chips,
steak and ale pies, hand-battered pollock
thickens the air and there are Cumberland sausages
smothered nibbles and sharers to tide us over.

I know that the birthday girl wears a pink rosette
jelly babies are an essential cocktail ingredient
and the wrong kind of Sambuca selfie shot
can be a horror.

I know that the lairy lads in the next booth mean no harm
but they're shipping in the next round
betting on the next goal
first bloke to get the new girl's number.

I know that County lost again today
and Cloughie is a city hero forever.

I know this city.
I know the late bus will be lively
and someone drunk will kick off
about something on the journey.

But, most importantly, I know that,
when they reach their stop,
the people will always
thank their driver—
unless, of course, they're strangers.

GREY CITY WAGTAILS

Late night drinkers spill from The Bell into a raw
evening on Market Square. Those out to settle
old scores stumble below our ghostly
backlit plane tree, all alone since new tracks
felled its sisters and the tram's unceasing groan began.

Although still winter, our dove-grey lemon plumage
gives this perch an appearance of Spring.
Not that anyone down there would notice or expect to find us
here in such unusual habitat. They scurry
for sanctuary, brains addled by beer, bodies cooling
while we, warmed by sky cuisine,
roost from dusk to dawn in our silent hundreds.

WHITEBEAM

Your whitebeam has lost its breezy
grey-green mystery, its soft, high summer curves
before you had the chance to know them.
Thrushes will no longer sing in secret nor
squirrels leap through its limbs to scramble
across half-glimpsed walls beyond.
Your builder said he was thinning out the tree
to let in more light but half an hour of chainsaw
anarchy ransacked its sanctuary
exposing you to more clatter and traffic.
All comfort has gone: its stumps cast
stunted shadows over your dry lawn
strewn with leaves.

GOING NOWHERE

A long queue in damp dark
for the 'due' but not yet spotted number 17.
No-one waits on the cold metal bench.

A woman on her mobile to the daughter
she'll be seeing later anyway.
Two overweight men agree that
Bitcoin isn't money laundering.
A nurse nurses her e-book.
A boy waits without a coat.
A couple tut about unsuitable clothing.

A mixture of *All Days* and *Kangaroos* get on
along with singles, passes and those chancing their arm
to use concessionary rates in peak time.
There is no drinking, no eating, no smoking,
no loud music and no priority seat left
for anyone who can't stand.

People perched on flip downs
flip them up for Pushchair Mum
struggling with a dodgy brake pedal while
the bus chugs us all up hill
towards home or work or
wherever.

Before anyone is really settled
Bobble Hat Drunk starts his abuse.
Feet up on a double seat
head leaning on the window
he cranks up his observations.

We try to take our minds elsewhere
look for that long-lost thing
at the bottom of bags
send texts we must send

scan an unread *Metro*
stare anywhere but at him.

Except one.

She
calls him *a racist*
challenges his violent intentions
his verbal assault on a woman's hijab
on her crying baby
and their right to be
on the bus
with us
with him.

Others get braver now
tell him *Shut up.*
Keep quiet.
Shut the fuck up!
Leave the bus.
Get out!
Wait outside.
Walk home.

The bus stops.
A tired father watches his toddler
throw toys.
Others will be late for their shifts
their match, dinner, visitor or
regular home-time chat with a friend.

Bobble Hat has his feet up.
Going nowhere.

Our driver remains calm.
We think the police are coming.

'NO VALVE TOO SMALL'

The Valve Shop, Radford, Nottingham
(for Elaine)

Is that The Valve Shop?
Yes, madam.
I need a replacement valve.
Would that be for a hot tap, cold tap, cooker or barbeque?
No.
A washing machine, washer–dryer, dishwasher or gas boiler?
No.
A two-stroke engine, trumpet, French horn or tuba?
No.
Submersible, furnace or rotary feeder?
No.
Dust-buster?
No.
Is it a gate, plug, globe or check valve you're after?
No
Butterfly or rotor?
No.
Diaphragm or ball?
No.
Two-way or three-way?
Not sure.
It's for a heart.

Now would that be living or artificial?
The heart?
The valve.
What's the difference?

Well, your living valve anticipates
hæmo-dynamic events
changes its shape and size
responds to pressure
as the red stuff pulses round your system.

Your artificial valve is more open and shut,
more of a portcullis really
oblivious to changes in pressure,
needs help to let off steam.

Which would you advise?
It depends.
On what?
How they sound.
What?
Your lub and dub?

My…?
Your sequences of lub and dub
your first and second heart sounds:
your blood flowing against different valves—
the ones that are working that is.

'Course you could have more sounds.
I could?

Or they could be split, murmuring or even galloping.
Tell you what, why don't you give 'em all a listen—
that'll help me search through the right boxes at any rate.
Can I call you back in a minute
once I've sorted out this rush order?

THE 9TH DUCHESS OF RUTLAND AS A SKETCH

(after Laura Knight, 1934)

In watercolour, chalk and wash
she is a younger, lighter
less daubed
less doughty version of her oiled self.

Heavy curtains do not swamp or
smother her morning in dark velvet.
Instead a leafy backdrop stirring
in the breeze from an unseen window
gives her body airy potential.

She is unencumbered
save for a long flick of pearls.
Evening garments lift and swish.
Thick rings and a heavy brooch
destined for her final self
are absent.

Johnnie (the family bulldog
who requires separate sittings)
does not guard the family jewels with bared teeth
does not anchor her.

This duchess could float away.

ARBORETUM SHAPES

6th July 2016

Between… among… through
in… under… over the green space
people are making their own shapes.

One knee bent forward
a cyclist anchors his bike to the lawn
sits cradled in its slight shadow
head fixed on middle distance.

Stretching her body flat
beneath the soft-leaved Foxglove tree
the reader turns slow white pages above grass
tries to lose herself in words.

The nurse ignores her fob watch
for a few final minutes, drains a coke
forms a triangle with elbow, hand and mobile
for a breathy Spanish chat.

A family arrange pushchair, rug, picnic.
Young Dad and partner draw in the breezy calm
lose themselves in the newborn
gurgling at their centre.

Four young men celebrate Eid
ambling round the park perimeter
photograph ancient specimens
exchange shy jokes in cool shade.

An office worker, tie loosened,
pauses over his takeaway
to stare for a moment into
an unknown somewhere.

Mum, friend and toddler emerge
from a dark tunnel crescent into light.
Toddler chomps on melon slices
wriggles in his harness

desperate to run along the winding path
towards clown-faced birds and a gardener
clipping rims of the circular
borders with her long-handled shears.

THE TRAIN MAN: EDDIE ISAAC MBE

I never knew your name
till the day you retired
but I heard your whistle
its shrill insistence
cutting through the fug of announcements
The train now standing on platform 2...
East Midlands Trains apologises for the delay
We are sorry to announce....
Market Harborough, Kettering, London St. Pancras

Eddie Isaac in your high-viz
with your peaked black cap
smartly knotted tie

Stand clear of the moving train
Will passengers on platform 3...
This train does not stop here
Syston, Sileby, Barrow-on-Soar

Eddie always ready to
welcome
urge
not in company-speak
(no *platformed* trains for you)
but on-the-hoof *let's be having you,*
haven't you got homes to go to?
banter with locals,
commuters, trainspotters at platform ends
a song, a joke, a smile
while you mind the doors
keep the timetable moving

A 'Leicester legend'
you breakfast on raw eggs
fuelled by your desire to serve

Welcome to Leicester
You are so welcome to Leicester

The Queen told you
no-one will ever break your record
53 years working on the rail

Chill wind might blow up the platform
rain lash along the platform
long shadows creep across the platform
but you were there every day
always blowing that whistle

REALTOR REALITY

She doesn't want to go back to Saskatchewan
needs to ship out, refocus, move on.

The realtor tries to put a price on her life
starts to negotiate, consider *with respect*
the logistics of business transfer
ask *with respect* what sum,
based on future projections, she was thinking.

She will not sell herself cheap
could wait out another year
fills the café with talk of *custom designed tee-shirts, trademarks,*
over fifty franchises province-wide.

He wants her numbers and *with respect*
only then could he work something out.
140, 150, 190K—what does she think?
240, 250, 290K—what could she make?

Projections are projections
but she gives nothing away
knows there are *a million wannabe Jesses out there*
and she's not one of them.

Snatches of Beethoven compete with
chairs squeaking on linoleum
forks scratching across stoneware
short order calls for salmon on whole wheat
a woman pleading for no eggs, no bread, no dairy
children screaming to see the blue whale.

He needs to look again
taps imaginary numbers once more.

She needs to think again
takes hard stiletto steps towards the door.

THEY EAT BEANS MOSTLY

'they eat beans mostly, this old yellow pair'
(from: *The Bean Eaters* by Gwendolyn Brooks)

Thunderstorms they
had not foreseen jinxed the lovers' plans to eat
late breakfasts outdoors then harvest ripened beans
before the summer was, mostly,
done with its dry warmth. But now there was this
charged atmosphere and the feeling that old
Autumn would soon throw his yellow
net completely over them, the sometimes happy pair.

THE WAY HE LIVED NOW

'With his great white strong cold squares of teeth'
(from *the vacant lot* by Gwendolyn Brooks)

She knew there was trouble with
the way he lived now when she ventured into his
garden again, saw the creeping speedwell, great
purple thistles instead of bean poles, white
dead-head nettles colonising borders with their strong
nicotine-fingered roots and the empty cold
frames where seedlings in serried squares
once waited for the next stage of
propagation but she could only pull weeds, grit her teeth.

                    S l o w l y
          b r e a k i n g **n** a r r o w l e a v e s
w h i t e h o o d s p u s h t h r **o** u g h
                    r a **w**
                    i c e **d**
                            g **r** o u n d
          b r i n g i n g u s h **o** p e
                    t h a t s **p** r i n g w i l l
                            s o o n f o l l o w

GARDENING WITH MATTHEWS

(from *Garden with Matthews: volume 2* by J.W. Matthews)

Every gardener can be a plant improver
but growth can be harmful.
Boronia's enemies kill
homely swede with kindness
or wetter water.

When hedges become undesirable
when walnuts do not fruit
when sweet peas drop their buds
the Kōwhai lament.

AT ROSE'S PARTY

Hammond's Arboretum 1928

His Majesty
Prince de Bulgarie
General MacArthur
Commandant Félix Faure
The Duchess of Wellington
The Countess of Longsdale
Baroness Rothschild
Lady Pirrie
Lady Rachiquin
Captain Kilbee Stuart
The Prior of Colchester
Miss Alice Rothschild
Mrs Tresham Gilbey
Mrs Wemys Quin
Mrs Oakley Fisher
Mrs Henry Bowles
Mrs Amy Hammond
Madame Edouard Herriot
Madame Abel Chantenay
Mrs Cutbush
Miss Beatty
Common Miss Clibraus
Caroline Testout
Florence Izzard
Dorothy Howarth
Augustus Hartman
Norman Lambert
Donald MacDonald
Phoebe, hiding behind Collins,
Padre
and Ma Fiancée.

HE KNOWS THE SOUND

He knows every sound water makes
pouring from butt to can:
that initial hollowness
followed by tinny echoes
along metal base and rim.

Without ever needing to look
he senses imminent fullness
when thickening liquid eases
towards gaping mouth and spout.

In that second he
thrusts spade into soil
turns off the tap.

CROCKS

brilliant green teapot spout
spiral patterned side plate

sturdy stoneware squeezer
white porcelain butter dish

daisy bordered cake stand
soft purple sweet pea vase

rose stencilled sugar bowl
Crown Derby coffee cup

blue speckled breakfast mug
much loved minute milk jug

hidden cracked histories

HOW TO SURVIVE ABOVE THE CLOUDS

(Mount Teide National Park, Tenerife)

Resist tough extremes of temperature
by reducing exposure.
Cover your leaves with downy hairs,
beeswax or similar.

Adopt hemispherical forms,
rosettes or a pillow shape
to provide greater protection
for your most delicate interior parts.

Sport bright coloured flowers
(hot red, canary yellow,
dazzling white and violet are popular)
to attract pollinating insects and birds.

Release a large volume of seeds
into thin mineral soil
or disperse them to the winds
to enhance your chances of reproduction.

Find out how others develop
their ability to survive in adversity
and learn to thrive
on our harsh high mountains.

ASTROPHYSICISTS

They are a breed apart
the astrophysicists:
thirty heads living in transparent skies
among silver-blue brightness
where residual snow tricks visitors
into a false sense of warmth.

They ignore earthly matters
preferring to draw zodiacal light
down forty-six metre telescopes
pore over refracted images, solar granules
dissect sunspots, time-lapse deep space,
peruse brown dwarfs in three dimensions.

They were sleepy at first
the astrophysicists
but thrive now in high altitude,
bodies aligned to star rhythms.
After lunch they will revisit
microwaves from the Big Bang
catch its last millisecond.

HOW TO HANDLE A NEW YEAR

Rake each month to a fine tilth
drag the flints, broken glass,
empty snail shells to one side
reveal the black earth
touch its teeming friable places

Look at the stars properly for once
name their constellations with confidence
call them up from darkest skies
Andromeda, Cygnus, Cassiopeia, Orion,
hear their songs humming beyond light

If all else fails
cross and re-cross
the Date Line
queue up for seconds
eat them carefully

LAUNDE ABBEY LOSS

(for Raminder)

All at once there was no-one.
Everyday.
It was a hard lesson.
No longer anyone to share.
The laughter was gone.

She wants to lose her loss
loosen its ties
but keep their bond tight
freed from pain
live on
not leave him
not forget him
pass through sadness
into different sadness.

For a moment, she is there again
with an unknown other,
another loser with an unspoken story.

They both know it will never be the same.
They can never be the same.
They can never go back.

RAIN FALLING DAYS

rain falling days

head buffeted
hair lashed by dragon wind

days falling dark

head stormed
sleep tossed in night rigging

rain falling days

head drenched
dreams flooded by rain tongue

days falling dark falling rain falling days

BULRUSH

Bullish bold rust-brown battalions, your
unflinching leathery leaves are a
last line of defence against the fluid
rim where you
usurp others' reflections
stir, sigh, stand to attention
hide so much beneath and beyond
edges of your watery
secret hinterlands.

VISUAL LITERACY

Bunched hair, bare feet and legs too short to touch the floor,
the young girl in the front row has good stationery
a clutch of pens, a smiley spiral-bound notebook, a stack of post-its
spread out on her study desk.

She fashions an iPad from red and yellow post-its
uses pink stickers for buttons
fills her yellow screen with busy images.

She is a seasoned conference-goer
watches Mum hold up her shiny device
to capture a reference or photograph
a slide of bullet points about effective writing
and young people's lack of literacy skills.

The young girl holds her paper tablet aloft,
angles it to the projected presentation
presses each pink button in turn.

She glances around, writes notes to herself in Arabic.
Do they remind her of what she has seen?
Are they for a poem, a report or a new story?

With her bunched hair, bare feet and legs too short to touch
       the floor,
she smiles when Mum asks a question
sizes up the speaker
waits for his response.

Through the classroom window
Dad makes driving signals
points left towards the car park.
She knows
she will be able to leave soon.

BRIDESMAIDS AT CANA

(after Stanley Spencer, 1935)

Pre-wedding babble bubbles.
Overlapping thighs writhe
bent-over bums perch
sturdy shiny legs cross then uncross
with the occasional petticoat
or stocking-top showing.
Feet snuggle plumply inside fur-lined slippers
lounge on pouffes, low-slung settees
snooze in saggy reading chairs.

Sucking away waiting hours
beige-brown frocked bridesmaids
and their hangers-on engross
themselves in newspapers
gossip about whether *Joan will make a scene*
or Reg has been invited
after all that went on
wonder if she'll wear ivory or cream
Crêpe-de-Chine or satin
whether there'll be enough wine.

Under the dining table a child
stretched out on deck
flips through a fabric book
sets sail on her adventures.

IN PRAISE OF THE PENCIL SHARPENER

Since Primary school she'd marvelled
at mechanisms that accommodated
different diameters, grades of hardness
or doubled as rubbers.

Shaving thin and RicRac reveal
were main attractions alongside
list-making, sketching,
sharpening words to a point.

She didn't admire those
masquerading as movie creatures
but dreamed of stationery nirvana:
a deluxe, no-mess, no-nonsense electric version.

Enthusiasm dimmed when it dawned on her
such snug fit and twist, twirled
tension of graphite and wood against blade
would be replaced by an instant buzzing incision.

There'd be no need for deft wrist movement
nor a serrated lens eye to grip each
gleaming Palamino, striped Staedtler, Derwent,
Cumberland or coloured Caran d'Ache.

Electric versions lacked elegance compared
with the handsome classroom sharpener
bolted to teacher's desk with its sawdusty
compartment for discarded skirts in all shades.

This was the one everybody always
volunteered to empty: a duty,
teacher said, for which you had to wait.

It was never her turn.

END OF A DAY AT THE POOL

Pool guards lower umbrellas
straighten beds
deflate lilos
leave swimmers
sleepers
readers
to themselves.

Sun slips beneath horizon islands
pages flick
while the cool pool laps at my back.

That small girl, who splashed
and squealed all afternoon,
now knows her books
can't float on water.

DOES THIS POEM PAY ITS WAY?

The UK Government's Culture Secretary Maria Miller said the arts world must make the case for public funding by focusing on its economic, not artistic, value (BBC News 24/4/13)

While reading or listening to this poem you should decide
if it gives you value for money.
Please tick or indicate all that apply.

Does it:

a) reap the reward of your reading investment time?
b) merit further reading investment?
c) make you want to read the poet's new collection?
d) persuade you to investigate the poet's back catalogue?
e) stimulate the wider literary economy through purchase of:
   - tickets for readings
   - CD recordings
   - poetry apps
   - library memberships (only available to purchase)
   - works of criticism
   - stationery items
   - visits to writers' houses
   - computer hardware
   - office furniture or back supports
   - magazine subscriptions
   - competition entry fees
   - a shed to write in
   - a writing retreat/holiday
   - editorial support
   - copying, printing or binding facilities
   - the services of an amanuensis
   - a waste paper bin?

KEEPERS OF THE ABBEY

We can't replace,
re-plaster, re-varnish, repair, restore
but we can recycle pheromone traps
trace silverfish, carpet beetles and
woodworm with trails
of deadly eggs.

We can't clean Calke Abbey muck
but can glean the skin
of those coming in
since 1985.

We can't polish and preserve
but can conserve rust
dab and dust
in shifts of three staff
over four years.

Personally, I can't get excited
about mould or the holes
moths make
but I can tell you about
insect infestations
and I do know that blue
fades first
no matter how
we keep light low
trap air flow
watch under microscopes
each summer's passing.

DOLLIES

I

Mum's 'heirloom' was porcelain
with hard eyes
cold, breakable limbs.
Permanently dressed
in a white christening gown
she was nameless, not a toy.

Smothered in baby pink and frilly lace
plastic Mandy bleated her arrival
on my fourth birthday.
She could not wet like *Tiny Tears*
but I liked her pram with its quilted
coverlet to conceal a book beneath.

Patty, a walking, talking model,
wore a bright red tunic.
She never walked or talked much -
her batteries constantly borrowed
for adventures involving
space travel, walkie-talkie radios.

Sindy was the sophisticated friend
with her striped weekender top, blue swimsuit,
outfits for dancing, dressage and dates with Paul.
She could prance in front of a three-way mirror all she liked
but she'd never party with Barbie
owned by girls on the other side of town.

II

You had to hide your dolly
in a drawer
in a house
in a country
where your family used to live.

It has ruby lips
blue eyes.
You want it back.

TESTING THE WATER

She does handstands on the sand
moulds wet gloop into pies
surprised by the grittiness
coating her fingers.

She learns to dig
makes moats and tunnels,
fortifications and bucket-shaped towers,
plants yellow flags with a lion rampant.

She runs over shiny rivulets
hard at first then soft,
toes beginning to tingle at
first touch of afternoon sea.

TOITŪ TE WHENUA

Whatungarongaro te tangata toitū te whenua
As man disappears from sight, the land remains (Māori proverb)

Leave it to honey-coloured light
bathing your Hokianga hills

Leave it to tall, tall eucalypts
peeling russet rasps of bark

Leave it to chests of unnamed stars
pulsing above peninsulas

Leave it to bottlenose dolphins
curving air, chasing bow waves

Leave it to iridescent clams
slipping eels, green-lipped mussels

Leave it to boisterous tui
flitting fantails, liquid warblers

Leave it to wide rivers
roaring their ancient songs

WHALE GRAVEYARDS

I

Skegness, Lincolnshire, UK

After a stranding
sperm whales are no longer
Crown Property nor material for corsets.

Trophy hunters commit offences
hack at bodies, steal teeth, bones
daub graffiti, take selfish selfies.

Undernourished mammals collapse,
shrink, belch gas and, when poked,
slump to empty barrage balloons.

A digger hauls their remains away
for marine scientific investigation.

II

Farewell Spit, South Island, NZ

After a stranding
Karakia are sung at beach burial sites.

Tangaroa, Guardian of the Sea
is thanked for his koha.

Huge jawbones and teeth are cut out,
immersed in sea water, bleached by sun.

Taonga are carved
for the iwi, for the wharenui.

Traditions
keep the life force strong.

BROKEN

Hairline cracks lay concealed
beneath gleaming celadon.

With each small vibration
clay weakens
                        gaps widen
until
multiple scars need repair.

Perhaps they could be patched with gold
healed by urushi's lacquer
kintsugi's shine.

Or they could part forever,

let new light
into empty spaces.

ORANGES

You brought us four
from your Ehime home town
a welcome gift wrapped in cellophane.

We nodded, said our best *arigatos*
but didn't know until we peeled them
smelled their rare perfume
separated each delicate segment
savoured such intense sweetness
how special they were.

We shared one at a time
twilight at Itsukushima Shrine
a Shinkansen ride to Kobe
wandering in Kyoto's ordered gardens
on the Thunderbird Express through
mountains thick with snow.

Delicious Beni-Madonna
magic Beni-Madonna
fizzing with flavour.
Other fruit seem ordinary now.

AT RYOANJI TEMPLE

At the entrance, a tour guide tells her group
they will now visit a small garden
with some rocks and gravel.
She says she can't begin to explain it
but she will try.

One of their party wants to know
who rakes the ground
who keeps the place tidy.

An American child is adamant
there are only fourteen rocks.
She will not be argued with:
she knows what she can see.

They don't linger on the bare wooden boards
of a veranda worn shiny by so many slippered feet
and therefore miss a brief slant of winter sunlight
through the blind of pines
falling diagonally across fifteen seen
and unseen rocks
all fringed with moss
lapped by a white sand sea.

WHAT THEY LEFT BEHIND

A lunchbox
A watch
An artificial eye

An anonymous vase
A personal seal
A national flag

A train pass
A bank book
A child's dress

A wooden sandal
A belt buckle
A pair of trousers

Her uniform
His tricycle
Her daughter's hair

Noburu Sunada's canteen
Futoshi Tanimoto's mess kit
His mess kit cover

Sentaro Akinobu's binoculars
for viewing cherry blossoms
on Hijiyama Hill

m i s t a k e

m j t u b l f

m k t v c m g

m l t w d n h

m m t x e o i

m n t y f p j

m o t z g q k

m p t a h r l

m q t a i s m

m r t a j t n

m s t a k u o

m t t a l v p

m u t a m w q

m u t a n x r

m u t a o y s

m u t a p z s

m u t a q a s

m u t a r b s

m u t a s c s

m u t a t d s

m u t a t e s

SPELLING IT OUT

You make the beginning of
every internal word.
You are metaphor and reality.
Three letters tell
my ribosomes to spell
out protein pearls
string together
a thousand amino acids
inside each beautiful bead.

Although you always dazzle folk
with your sexy flexing chain
somewhere along my
twisting untwisting
zipping unzipping ladder
you made a mistake.

When did this happen:
1962, 1932, 1898…?

Where does my error lie?
Upstream or downstream?

And what were my odds?
50: 50?
50: 50?
50: 50?
50: 50?

One wrong letter.

Is the miscreant A or T:
Adenine or Thymine?

G or C:
Guanine or Cytosine?

One wrong letter.
Proliferating.

UNDRESS

There is no mystery now:
you can *all* look if you want to.

No need for modesty either
nor a swish of concealing curtain
each time I remove my clothes
while you hurry through your medical terms
take tentative measurements
press my undressed uncertain flesh.

SMALL TALK

I sense that some things
can be talked about
but a miniscule look
exchanged across the dining table
between those I love most
tells me that others
have moved into a
never-ever
off-the-scale
no-speak zone
of chats we would could should have
now
or at any time in the future.

FURIOUS ANSWERS

(after *The Answer is No*, Kay Sage, 1938)

The answer is definitely NO!
I don't want a hopeless sky
layered with dark greys
diffusing to pale teal
on the near horizon.

I don't want my view squared off
limited and restricted
by blank, silent or un-stretched canvas.

I need hope
sunlight, nuances of shade.

I want colour
nature
humanity.

I want
contesting
contrasting
startling
arresting
uplifting
questioning
visions.

I need painters, photographers
carvers and engravers,
collagists and ceramicists
weavers and wordsmiths
with their delicious,
curious,
furious answers
to burst from the frames,
to set my mind on fire.

MEDICAL HUMANITIES

Before
taking temperature
testing urine
drawing blood
measuring pulse
hearing heart
marking skin
inserting cannula
masking up
cutting through
please listen
to my mind.

PRESENT

You contort your body to conceal
what will soon be missing.

You try to lean nonchalantly
on one elbow
use a hand to hide your balding head.

You are one of very many
called by a name you never use.

You could slip into a dark interior
at any moment if you chose.
You choose not to.

For now you are unbowed,
present.

Your right breast twists
out of shape but you *are* here
still here in the light.

SLIP

A normal day
no longer exists.
You feel yourself slipping
sidling between selves inside outside.

Not that anyone can see.
If they listened hard they might.
Then they'd shoot you an unspoken
there for the grace of God kind of look
but you can't dwell on that
or you'd slip further.

As it is you're still trying
to scale an iceberg,
holding on somewhere
below the waterline.

11 ROUNDS

1.
She says I have good veins
searches for *a bouncy one*.
It blows then blooms to
quick blackness around my wrist.

2.
The cold cap is freezer fresh
and squeaks over scalp.
A headache threatens but
my lover straps me in for the next round.

3.
Brown plastic wrappers conceal
rate checked, rechecked, drip-fed drugs
shield them from late afternoon sun
in our stuffy day case bay.

4.
The nurse watches a red liquorice snake
slowly discharge its poison.
It is good;
she cannot give me an antidote.

5.
Each ice cube is an iceberg
scraping the walls of my mouth.
It cannot roll over or reveal its full size.
It will make me gag. It does.

6.
My thirst cannot be sated.
I must sip and sip and
sip and sip water, and
long for an everlasting daiquiri.

7.
My brain can only handle one piece
of your interesting news at a time.
I sift present, try not to delve into past,
learn to keep future on hold.

8.
And my tongue is a livid salamander
mired in hot mucous.
Its sandpaper surface mixes
saliva with thick wallpaper paste.

9.
And my sweating neck sinks
into steamy pillows.
Night clothes cling to wet skin
between tropical sheets.

10.
Early mornings have a different rhythm
now I have no buses or trains to catch.
I am in my seat waiting
for the blackbirds' dawn call.

11.
I wobble then try to stride—
wrestle, resist, forget, remember.
I wobble then try not to stumble
along the edge of days.

HOCKNEY SPRING

Five years ago, home from
Auckland's Autumn typhoons and flapping flax
you gave me back a Spring I had not seen—
the leap from bare flame hawthorn to burst hedge,
soft pink-red campion taking undergrowth by stealth
ground thick with ramsons,
froth of shepherd's purse and celandine brilliance,
ghostly foxgloves sentinel in green-dark
and a fanfare of leaves with lives of their own
dancing
      dazzling
           unfurling
                in dappled light
between branches.

And now, my mouth furred with chemo
head blurred by those endless winter hours
of night checks, drain bottles,
infections, cannulas and scarred skin,
you jolt me back up to earth once more
edging out gloom with fervent colour,
colour that makes sound,
drives starlings to shout and shimmer in treetops.

Your ruby-mauve road still leads tunnel-wards
but this time I can see how fast it's running.

FRIENDS WALKING FRIENDS TALKING

(for Rob and Sarah)

In blue-skied afternoons
we walk along ancient oak-lined lanes
hedgerows thick with yellow archangels
and waxy alexanders.

You speak over and
            under
              each other
break into
       argument/laughter
       laughter/argument.

Wood anemones tilt tiny star heads
towards sunlight
           slanting
               through
                    birches
and the promise of bluebells.

You are loud and soft
impatient and mindful
loving and testing
all at the same time.

Unseen at first
early dog violets creep
           sweet purple
              out into the open among
                  bright gorse
                  dried last of winter grasses.

You never finish sentences but give
different angles on hard memories

leave spaces for me to fill
or say nothing.

We come up for air where curlews call
across saltmarsh, bleached skeleton trees
stand eerie sentinel, drones chase
startled seagulls

silence us

NOTES

Page 27: Gardening with Matthews

Kōwhai: a native tree of New Zealand with bright yellow flowers

Page 47: Whale graveyards

Karakia: prayers or incantations
koha: gift
taonga: treasures
iwi: tribe
wharenui: Māori meeting house

Page 48: Broken

urushi: a natural lacquer and adhesive used in decoration or repair of ceramics
kintsugi: a Japanese method of repairing broken ceramics